SHARKS
ON THE
HUNT

Thanks to the creative team:
Senior Editor: Alice Peebles
Fact Checking: Tom Jackson
Illustration: Dan Newman
Picture Research: Nic Dean
Design: Perfect Bound Ltd

Hungry Tomato®
A division of Lerner Publishing Group, Inc.
241 First Avenue North
Minneapolis, MN 55401 USA

For reading levels and more information, look up
this title at www.lernerbooks.com.

Main body text set in Avenir Next Condensed Medium 11/15.
Typeface provided by Linotype AG.

Library of Congress Cataloging-in-Publication Data

Names: Mason, Paul, 1967– author.
Title: Sharks on the hunt / Paul Mason.
Description: Minneapolis : Hungry Tomato, [2018] | Series: Wild world of
sharks | Audience: Age 8–12. | Audience: Grade 4 to 6. | Includes index.
Identifiers: LCCN 2017026114| ISBN 9781512459753 (lb) | ISBN
9781512498776 (ebk pdf)
Subjects: LCSH: Sharks—Juvenile literature.
Classification: LCC QL638.9 .M29 2018 | DDC 597.3/3—dc23

LC record available at https://lccn.loc.gov/2017026114

Manufactured in the United States of America
1-43034-27703-7/31/2017

SHARKS
ON THE
HUNT

by Paul Mason

HUNGRY
TOMATO®
Minneapolis

CONTENTS

SHARKS: APEX PREDATORS   6

WHAT SHARKS EAT   8

FINDING PREY   10

HUNTING BY SIGHT   12

HUNTING BY TOUCH AND TASTE   14

ELECTRO-LOCATION   16

HIGH-SPEED ATTACKERS   18

SHARK AMBUSHES   20

JAWS OF DEATH   22

TERRIBLE TEETH   24

SHARK MIGRATIONS   26

SEVEN INCREDIBLE SHARK FACTS   28

SHARK IDENTIFICATION   30

GLOSSARY   31

INDEX   32

SHARKS: APEX PREDATORS

Several big sharks are apex predators, scared of nothing. They are eating machines. Almost everything about sharks is designed for catching and consuming food.

The bull shark will eat just about anything that comes its way—including, rarely, humans. Fortunately, it *usually* eats fish.

BULL SHARK

*Unlike most sharks, bull sharks can survive in **fresh water**. Some live fulltime in a lake in Australia, having swam there during a flood!*

The goblin shark is sometimes called a "living fossil." It is the last survivor of a family of sharks that first appeared roughly 100 million years ago.

Bull sharks are common in shallow water near the coast. They sometimes gather in packs.

SHARKS EVERYWHERE

Our oceans are full of sharks. Wherever there is prey to eat, you find sharks hunting. Down in the gloom of the deep oceans, for instance, lurks the goblin shark. Below the Arctic ice you might spot a Greenland shark. And lying camouflaged on the seabed off shores around the world are various species of angel shark.

WOLVES OF THE SEA

Sharks are sometimes called "wolves of the sea." This name started with blue sharks. It came from their habit of gathering in packs, then attacking when they found something that could be a meal. Blue sharks are not that fussy about what they eat—in 1942, one was even caught with a bottle of wine in its stomach!

SHARK SCIENCE: SHARK-OLOGY

Fossil discoveries show that sharks have been around for a long time. Shark ancestors first appeared over 400 million years ago. Modern humans, *Homo sapiens*, only appeared less than 200,000 years ago!

WHAT SHARKS EAT

There are about 450 shark species. Some will eat whatever they find, others specialize in one kind of prey. Most sharks prefer to eat other fish.

Sharks That Eat Just About Anything

Many big species—such as tiger sharks, bull sharks, blue sharks, and great white sharks—eat all kinds of things. They have all been found with strange items in their stomachs, including a suit of armor. (Experts are not 100% certain this story is true. It was recorded in the 1500s by a **naturalist** named Guillaume Rondelet.)

TIGER SHARK

Crazy Contents of Tiger Shark Tummies

Tiger sharks are nicknamed the "garbage cans of the sea." These are just a few of the crazy things that have been found in their tummies:

- An echidna (an Australian animal similar to a porcupine)
- A bag of money
- A chicken coop—with chickens inside
- Tom-tom drums
- A car licence plate

NOT ON THE MENU: HUMAN

One thing sharks DON'T eat is humans—or not very often. Only a few shark species have ever attacked people. For us, the most dangerous are the great white, bull shark, and tiger shark. A few other shark species have bitten people, but attacks on humans are almost always a case of mistaken identity.

Tiger sharks are not fussy eaters. This one is nibbling on some tasty camera equipment.

PICKY EATERS

Some sharks are adapted to eat special types of food. Basking sharks, whale sharks, and a species called the megamouth suck up tiny plankton and krill with their giant mouths. Mako and blue sharks use their great speed to catch fast-moving fish. Angel and zebra horn sharks even eat shellfish!

SHARK SCIENCE: WHAT IS A SHARK?

Things that make sharks different from other fish:

- Their skeleton is made of tough **cartilage**, not bone.
- They can only swim ahead, and many sharks have to keep swimming all the time to keep breathing.
- Their teeth are arranged in rows, which are always pushing forward to replace teeth that have been lost.

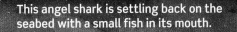

This angel shark is settling back on the seabed with a small fish in its mouth.

FINDING PREY

A fish or sea mammal that is bleeding is almost certain to attract sharks. Many sharks follow the smell of blood to find possible prey.

The part of a shark's brain used for smell is large. Sharks can follow a smell for hundreds of meters.

Sharks use special sensors on the underside of their snout to pick up scents. The sensors are called nares, and there is one on each side of the shark's snout.

Water flows into the hole at the top and out of the bottom.

LEMON SHARK

A shark can tell where a smell comes from. If the smell reaches its right nare before the left one, the shark knows the smell is coming from the right.

SNIFFING OUT PREY

It is not only the blood of wounded animals that sharks can smell. They can also sniff out healthy prey. According to the American Museum of Natural History, lemon sharks can detect just a teaspoon of fish oil in a swimming pool of water.

Some sharks, such as this blind shark, have barbels hanging down from their snouts. These are used to locate prey.

VIBRATIONS IN THE WATER

Sharks also detect prey from the sounds and vibrations made by struggling or injured fish. Sharks have ears at the sides of their head, though there is only a tiny hole on the outside. But they also have a much bigger system for sensing vibrations in the water. This is called the lateral line.

SHARK SCIENCE: THE LATERAL LINE

The lateral line is a line of sensors under a shark's skin, running down the side of its body. Along the line, a jelly-like substance wobbles whenever the water is disturbed. The wobbles trigger a message to the shark's brain. It says, "Something worth investigating is happening!"

HUNTING BY SIGHT

Sight is an important hunting tool for many sharks. Once they are close enough to see their prey, they use vision to close in for the kill.

This great white was moving so fast, it left the water completely and did a front flip!

ATTACKING FROM BELOW

Great white sharks rely on vision when attacking from below. When it is ready, the great white races straight up to the surface and hits the prey at full speed.

The shark swims underneath its prey, which is often a seal.

The seal is outlined against the light above and easy to see.

The seal is unlikely to spot the shark in the gloom below.

Seals are often stunned by the force of a great white's attack.

GREAT WHITE SHARK

Down here on the seabed, this seal is safe from attack. Unfortunately, though, she has to go up to the surface to breathe.

Great whites are thought to be able to swim up to 25 mph (40 km/h).

HUNTING AT NIGHT

Sharks have good vision in darkness. They can make the most of any available light. Hunting at night, dusk, or dawn is no problem. For the great white, this is a big advantage. Seals—which are its main prey—travel to their feeding grounds at night and return at dawn. Most other sharks also hunt at night.

SLEEPING SHARKS

Most sharks have to keep moving to breathe. They need a constant stream of water through their gills. Some sharks, though, are able to pump water while lying on the sea bottom. One of these is the sand tiger shark or grey nurse shark. After a tough night of hunting, sand tigers lie on the bottom and rest for the day!

SHARK SCIENCE: THE TAPETUM LUCIDUM

The reason sharks see well without much light is the tapetum lucidum. This is a special layer in their eyes behind the **retina**.

The tapetum lucidum works by reflecting light back to the retina. This means the retina gets extra light signals so the shark can see better in the gloom.

The photographer's light has lit up the tapetum lucidum of this bigeye houndshark.

HUNTING BY TOUCH AND TASTE

In cloudy water, a shark may not be able to see well enough to finish a hunt. Instead, it first uses touch, then taste.

SHALLOW WATER

When swimming in cloudy water, if a shark bumps into something that might be food, it bites. If the something turns out to *taste* like food too, the shark carries on with the attack. If not, it stops.

In shallow, cloudy water, **juvenile** sharks sometimes use their sense of touch to hunt for fish. As a result, humans sometimes get bitten by accident. In Florida, for example, the water is often made cloudy by surf. If sharks bump into a surfer's foot or hand, they bite to see if it's food. When they realize it's not prey, they swim off. Attacks like this are sometimes called "hit and run" attacks.

Young blacktip sharks like these grow up in shallow water near the coast. They are common from South Carolina to Texas.

Diver Rodney Fox shows his scars from a great white shark attack. The shark that attacked him was distracted by some fish he had caught, which probably saved his life.

BUMP AND BITE

Large sharks also use touch and taste to see if something is food. These sharks, though, bump into things with their snouts on purpose.

First the shark circles an interesting object. Then it swims up from behind and either bumps it or takes a test bite. If the object is edible—even if it is a human—a large shark may continue the attack. This style of hunting is called "bump and bite." Great whites and bull sharks are known to hunt in this way.

BLACKTIP SHARKS

SHARK SCIENCE: TOUCH-SENSITIVE TEETH

Sharks have lots of nerves in their skin that can sense touch. They also have touch-sensitive teeth.

Sharks obviously do not have hands to feel with. Instead, they use their teeth to investigate unknown objects. They sometimes start with what is a nibble to them. (It would not feel like a nibble to you!) Then they may bite harder.

ELECTRO-LOCATION

Electro-location is a shark's secret weapon in its hunt for prey. Even if it cannot smell, hear, see, or touch its prey, electro-location helps the shark find something to eat.

Finding Prey with Electricity

Electro-location uses tiny holes underneath a shark's snout, called the ampullae of Lorenzini. These let the shark sense anything nearby that is producing electricity. Even the tiny electrical force of a fish's heartbeat shows up.

In many sharks, the ampullae are most tightly packed near their mouth. This helps the shark sense its prey's final attempts to escape. Hammerhead sharks have the ultimate electro-location tools. Their wide snouts have space for thousands of ampullae.

This great hammerhead is swimming along using its hammer like a metal detector. It is not looking for buried treasure—it's trying to sense stingrays buried in the sand.

A buried stingray's body will give off tiny electrical pulses.

If the hammerhead senses a stingray, it pins it down with its hammer. The shark then bites chunks out of the stingray's wings until it dies.

This stingray is trying to hide in the sand—but he'd better hope a hammerhead doesn't come along.

Shark Deterrent!

For years people have wondered how to stop shark attacks. One way to do this is said to be by carrying a special device that gives off an electric field. Nine times out of 10, when the shark gets close, it senses the field and turns away.

For goblin sharks, as for other deepwater sharks, electro-location is one of the most important hunting tools.

HAMMERHEAD SHARK

Some hammerheads have been found with almost 100 stingray **barbs** in their hammers. It seems the stingray's sting does not bother the shark.

Shark Science: Ampullae of Lorenzini

The ampullae of Lorenzini are gel-filled **pores** in a shark's snout. The pores are lined with tiny, sensitive cells.

The electric field from other animals in the water is transmitted to the gel, and the cells detect it. They send a message that there is something alive right under the shark's nose.

HIGH-SPEED ATTACKERS

Some sharks specialize in hunting fast-swimming prey, such as tuna. Bluefin tuna can swim at over 35 mph (60 km/h)! To catch them, sharks have to be speedy too.

THE SPEEDIEST SHARK

The fastest shark of all is the shortfin mako, which hunts bluefish, tuna, and mackerel. It is difficult to measure a shark's speed, but it's claimed that makos can swim at over 43 mph (70 km/h). They sometimes travel so fast that they leap out of the water. Makos have been reported jumping 30 ft (9 m)—almost as high as the highest diving platform at the Olympic Games.

Compared to other sharks, the mako has a much larger tail relative to its body. This allows it to generate lots of speed.

SWIFT ATTACKS

Although the shortfin mako is the fastest shark, many others use speed in the final phase of an attack. After the mako, the next fastest sharks are the great white and the blue shark. Each of these is thought to be able to reach 25 mph (40 km/h) in short bursts of speed.

Like the mako, the blue shark has a long, slim shape designed for speed.

The jaw is longer than it is wide, which is good for grabbing fish at high speed.

SHORTFIN MAKO SHARK

The **dorsal fin** stops the shark from rolling as it swims and helps it change direction.

Compare the mako with the tiger shark on page 8. The mako's body is long and pointed, enabling it to shoot through the water like an arrow.

The dorsal fin and swept-back **pectoral fins** are low-drag, so they do not slow the mako down.

SHARK SCIENCE: HYDRODYNAMICS

Hydrodynamics is the science of how water flows. It is similar to aerodynamics, the science of air flow.

Aerodynamics says that a sleek supercar will be faster than a flat-fronted van. In the same way, a sleek shark is faster than a big, wide one.

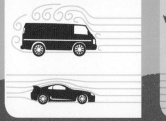

SHARK AMBUSHES

Few sharks hunt mainly by sight. The angel shark, though, lies in wait until it sees prey swimming past. Then, quick as a flash, it strikes!

A Big Family

There are about 20 members of the angel shark family, but they all hunt in a similar way. Their wide, flat bodies are perfect for lying camouflaged or hidden on the seabed. They wait in ambush until prey swims past. You can see how an angel shark lies in wait on the opposite page.

Lightning-Fast Strike

Once its ambush is ready, the angel shark waits until a fish comes just close enough. Sometimes the wait can last days. When a fish does swim within range, though, the angel shark's strike is almost too fast to see. Less than a tenth of a second after the attack has been launched, the fish is in the shark's mouth.

When hunting, the angel shark lies on the sandy seabed.

An angel shark's skin is just the right color to camouflage it in the sand.

The dorsal fins and tail lie flat, so that nothing sticks up to warn prey.

The shark wriggles down, hiding at least the edges of its body.

Nighttime Hunting

For a shark that relies on its vision to find prey, hunting at night seems an impossible challenge. But if no food comes along in daytime, the angel shark isn't defeated. It hunts at night using bioluminescence, the light trail created by fish as they swim.

Sometimes the shark covers itself almost completely, so that only its eyes and part of its head are exposed.

SHARK SCIENCE:
BIOLUMINESCENCE

Bioluminescence is light given off by some living things. It is the result of a chemical reaction.

The bodies of some fish are bioluminescent. Others leave a bioluminescent trail. As they swim along, these fish disturb tiny organisms in the water. The organisms give off bioluminescent light.

ANGEL SHARK

21

JAWS OF DEATH

Sharks' jaws are not like those of other animals. Their jaws work in a way that lets them take a MUCH bigger bite than you would expect. In fact, some sharks' jaws open almost as high and wide as their own bodies.

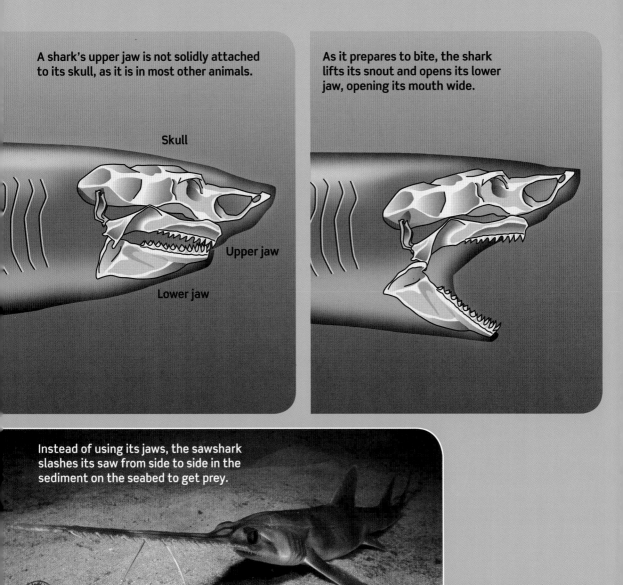

A shark's upper jaw is not solidly attached to its skull, as it is in most other animals.

Skull

Upper jaw

Lower jaw

As it prepares to bite, the shark lifts its snout and opens its lower jaw, opening its mouth wide.

Instead of using its jaws, the sawshark slashes its saw from side to side in the sediment on the seabed to get prey.

Big Mouths with No Bite

Not all sharks have a fearsome bite like a great white's. Two of the biggest—the whale shark and the basking shark—have huge mouths that rarely bite anything. Along with the incredibly rare megamouth shark, they are the only planktivorous sharks. This means that they live mainly off tiny sea creatures called plankton, which they suck up in their huge mouths.

A giant basking shark gulps down plankton while swimming lazily along.

The shark's upper jaw then moves away from its skull and pushes forward. This makes an even bigger bite. In some sharks, the opening movement sucks in water, dragging prey into their mouth.

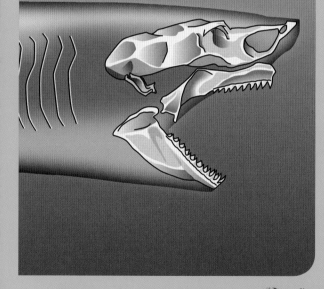

The upper and lower jaws snap together. A great white's bite is about as powerful as a lion's (and three times as strong as a human's), but its sharp teeth do massive damage.

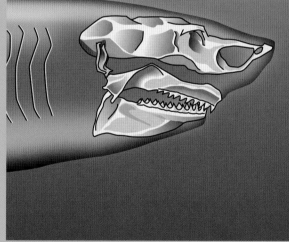

SHARK SCIENCE: BITE ID

When you bite into something, it leaves behind a pattern called a bite mark.

Every shark species has a different bite mark. The size and shape of their jaws and the position of their teeth are like a species fingerprint. A shark expert can often identify a shark just from its bite mark.

TERRIBLE TEETH

Sharks' teeth are frequently falling out and being replaced by new teeth from behind. Some sharks are thought to grow tens of thousands of teeth in a lifetime.

GREAT WHITE SHARK

Diet: Seals, sea lions, squid, and large fish

The great white has large, sharp, inward-leaning teeth. These allow it to hunt by taking a large bite from its prey, then waiting for it to bleed to death. If this does not happen, the shark attacks again, holding on and chomping at its victim.

PORT JACKSON SHARK

Diet: Shellfish and sea urchins

Sometimes called the oyster crusher, this shark feeds on shellfish, sea urchins, and other tough-to-eat animals. It uses its small, pointy front teeth to grab its prey. Then the Port Jackson's flat back teeth grind up its victim—a bit like a human chewing something tough.

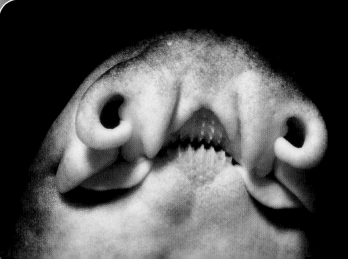

24

Sand Tiger Shark

Diet: Small bony fish, such as mullet and snapper

The sand tiger, also known as the grey nurse shark, feeds on small, fast-moving fish, so its teeth are shaped like rows of hooks. Once the shark bites down, it is almost impossible for a fish to escape.

Specialist Teeth

Each shark species has teeth that are adapted to the kind of prey it hunts. As sharks hunt almost anything that can be eaten, there are lots of different kinds of shark teeth. The four sharks shown here, though, have the four main kinds of teeth in the shark world.

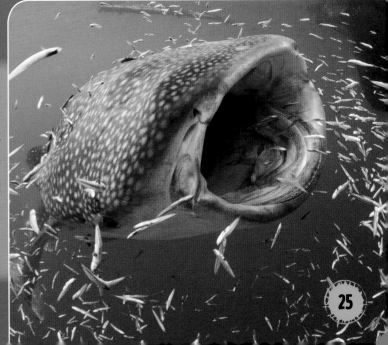

Whale Shark

Diet: Plankton and krill

Despite being the world's largest fish, the whale shark has no real need of teeth. It eats mostly tiny plankton and krill, which are swept into its giant mouth as it swims along. The shark does have rows of tiny teeth but does not use them for feeding.

SHARK MIGRATIONS

A migration is a journey from one feeding place to another. For some sharks, their whole life is a migration in search of food.

One of the great shark migrations happens when sharks follow sardine **shoals** up the coast of southeast Africa.

REGULAR MIGRATIONS

Some sharks return to the same places every year to hunt for food. Off the coast of southern Africa, for example, huge sardine shoals appear every June. The sharks know the sardines are coming and make sure they are waiting. In fact, sharks, dolphins, seabirds, and whales ALL come to feast on the sardines.

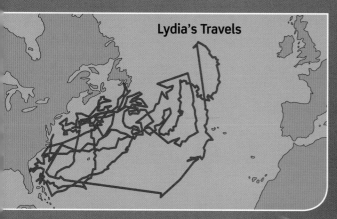

Lydia's Travels

CONSTANT MOTION

Some sharks are always on the move in search of food. They cover huge distances. In 2014, for example, a female great white was tagged off the coast of Florida. Lydia, as she was called, headed off along the east coast of North America. Then she set off across the Atlantic Ocean.

A year after being tagged, Lydia was in the eastern Atlantic, heading toward Cornwall in the UK. She had swum more than 18,500 miles (30,000 km).

Groups of sharks circle the ball of sardines. Bronze whalers, dusky sharks, silky sharks, and blacktip sharks are among the species that will attack the **bait ball**.

The sardines pack themselves together in a constantly moving ball. This makes it hard for predators to pick out a fish to attack.

SHARK SCIENCE: NAVIGATION

How do sharks find their way around? Scientists have several theories:

- Some, such as tiger sharks, seem to use the Earth's magnetic field as a kind of shark satnav.
- Other sharks may have memorized the area they inhabit.
- Sharks may also use ocean currents and water temperatures to tell them where they are.

SEVEN INCREDIBLE SHARK FACTS

1 Bull sharks hunt in rivers too

Most sharks are sea creatures, but bull sharks are able to survive in fresh water. In the United States, they have been caught hundreds of miles up the Mississippi River. In Africa, they were once called Zambezi sharks because they are so common in the Zambezi River.

2 Sharks start hunting even before they are born

Some sharks start hunting while they are still growing inside their mother. They attack and eat their smaller, weaker brothers and sisters.

3 Sharks give warnings that they are about to attack

Watching how a shark swims is a good guide to whether they might attack. Among the clues are swimming with an arched back, lowering the pectoral fins, making sudden changes of direction, and charging toward prey then veering off.

4 Orcas hunt sharks

Even the big boss of the shark world, the great white, is sometimes attacked—not by other sharks, but by **orcas**. The killer whales seem to see the sharks as a threat to their young. To orcas, great white shark liver is also a **delicacy**.

5 FEEDING FRENZIES DO HAPPEN

Most sharks hunt alone, though some species do hunt in packs. Sometimes, large numbers of sharks sniff out prey, such as a wounded or dead whale. The sharks begin to bite at anything that gets in their way, including each other. This is sometimes called a feeding frenzy.

6 THERE ARE NO VEGETARIAN SHARKS

All sharks are **carnivorous**, though some eat plants as well as meat. Sharks eat an amazing range of food—from tiny plankton to shellfish, fish, octopus, squid, birds, seals, and sea lions.

7 THE BIGGEST DANGER TO SHARKS IS HUMANS

In their world, most large sharks are apex predators. Nothing much attacks a large great white, for example—except an even larger great white. (See Fact 4 for the only exception.) But millions of sharks a year are killed by humans, mostly for their fins. Many of these are used in shark fin soup. Some experts think that for every human killed by a shark, up to 25 million sharks are killed by humans.

SHARK IDENTIFICATION

Scientists classify sharks in different groups according to their physical characteristics. This flow chart will help you identify some of the most commonly seen types of shark:

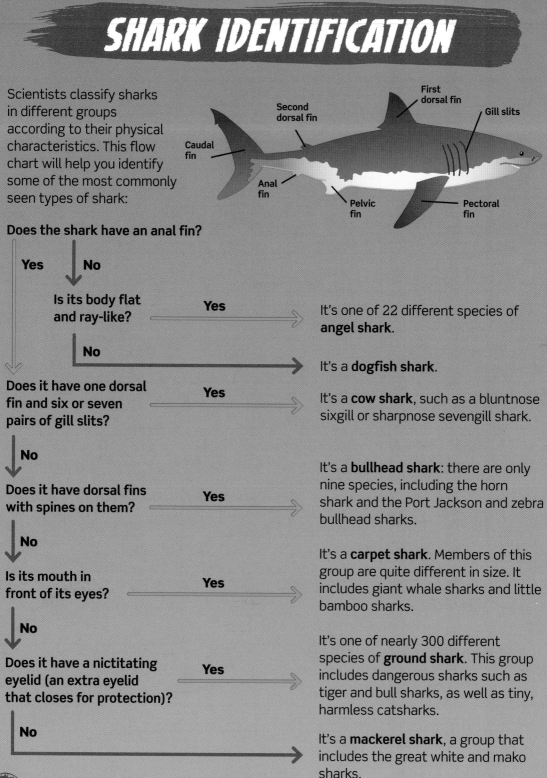

Second dorsal fin

First dorsal fin

Gill slits

Caudal fin

Anal fin

Pelvic fin

Pectoral fin

Does the shark have an anal fin?

Yes   **No**

Is its body flat and ray-like? — **Yes** → It's one of 22 different species of **angel shark**.

No → It's a **dogfish shark**.

Does it have one dorsal fin and six or seven pairs of gill slits? — **Yes** → It's a **cow shark**, such as a bluntnose sixgill or sharpnose sevengill shark.

No

Does it have dorsal fins with spines on them? — **Yes** → It's a **bullhead shark**: there are only nine species, including the horn shark and the Port Jackson and zebra bullhead sharks.

No

Is its mouth in front of its eyes? — **Yes** → It's a **carpet shark**. Members of this group are quite different in size. It includes giant whale sharks and little bamboo sharks.

No

Does it have a nictitating eyelid (an extra eyelid that closes for protection)? — **Yes** → It's one of nearly 300 different species of **ground shark**. This group includes dangerous sharks such as tiger and bull sharks, as well as tiny, harmless catsharks.

No → It's a **mackerel shark**, a group that includes the great white and mako sharks.

apex predator
an animal that is not hunted by any other animal

bait ball
a ball of numerous fish all swimming around and around close together. Forming a bait ball is a final defense by schools of fish against predators

barb
spike with a backward-pointing hook that lodges in skin

carnivorous (noun: carnivore)
an animal that only eats other animals

cartilage
strong, rubbery tissue that forms a shark's skeleton instead of bone; it makes sharks both lighter in weight and more flexible for their size than other fish

delicacy
food that is particularly tasty and a special treat

dorsal fin
the fin on a fish's back

fresh water
non-salty water in rivers and lakes

juvenile
young and not yet fully grown

naturalist
old name for someone interested in the world of nature; was an early kind of scientist

orca
largest member of the dolphin family, also known as a killer whale

pectoral fin
the fin on a fish's side, below and behind its head

pore
tiny opening in the skin

retina
layer of light-sensitive cells at the back of the eye

shoal
large group of fish swimming together

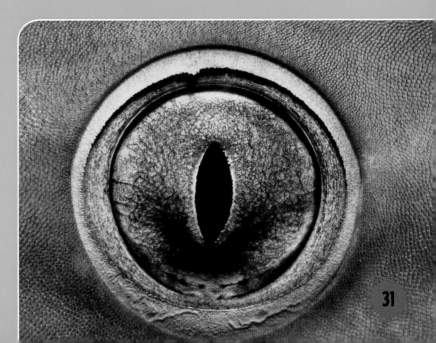

INDEX

ambushes, 20–21
ampullae of Lorenzini, 16–17
angel shark, 20–21

basking shark, 23
blacktip shark, 14–15
blind shark, 11
blue shark, 7, 18
breathing, 13
bullhead shark, 30
bull shark, 6–7, 28, 30

camouflage, 20
carpet shark, 30
cow shark, 30

electro-location, 16–17

feeding frenzy, 29
food, 8–9, 29
fossils, 7

goblin shark, 7, 17
great white shark, 18, 24, 28, 30
grey nurse shark, 13, 25
ground shark, 30

hammerhead shark, 16–17
humans
    attacks on sharks, 29
    shark attacks on, 9, 14–15
hydrodynamics, 19

jaws, 22–23

lateral line, 11
lemon shark, 10–11

mackerel shark, 30
migrations, 26–27

navigation, 27

Port Jackson shark, 24, 30

sand tiger shark, 13, 25
sawshark, 22
sense of smell, 10–11
sensing vibrations, 11
shortfin mako shark, 18–19
sight, 12–13
speed attacks, 18–19

tapetum lucidum, 13
teeth, 15, 24–25
tiger shark, 8–9, 30
touch and taste, 14–15

warning signs before attack, 28
whale shark, 25, 30
white shark, 12–14

ABOUT THE AUTHOR

Paul Mason is a prolific author of children's books, many award-nominated, on such subjects as 101 ways to save the planet, vile things that go wrong with the body, and the world's looniest inventors. Many of his books take off via surprising, unbelievable, or just revolting facts. Today, he lives at a secret location on the coast of Europe where his writing shack usually smells of drying wetsuit (he's a former international swimmer and a keen surfer).

Picture Credits

(abbreviations: t = top; b = bottom; c = centre; l = left; r = right)
Alamy: Carlos Villoch - MagicSea.com 20l; Cultura RM 2, 18, 28t; Dan Callister 12, 29t; Jeff Rotman 14bl, 24br, 31bl; Kelvin Aitken/VWPics 3, 9br, 17tr, 20bl; Mark Conlin 25tl; Nature Picture Library 1, 19tr, 24tl; Stephen Frink Collection 22bl; WaterFrame 6, 9tr. FLPA: Bruno Guenard/Biosphoto 13tr, 29b; Colin Munro 23tr; Fabien Michenet/Biosphoto 10; Flip Nicklin/Minden Pictures 21; Fred Bavendam/Minden Pictures 16bl; Gèrard Soury/Biosphoto 8, 16; Jeffrey Rotman/Biosphoto 11tr, 13; Patrice Heraud/Biosphoto 28b; Pete Oxford/Minden Pictures 26; Photo Researchers 15tr; Reinhard Dirscherl 4, 25br; Richard Herrmann/Minden Pictures 26t; Vincent Truchet/Biosphoto 14.
© www.shutterstock.com: Seashell World 23br.